Preparing for Motherhood

The Inside Scoop on Your New Job

Barbara Miller Juliani

www.newgrowthpress.com

New Growth Press, Greensboro, NC 27404
www.newgrowthpress.com

Cover Design: Faceout Books, faceout.com
Typesetting: Lisa Parnell, lparnell.com

ISBN-13: 978-1-938267-92-5
ISBN-13: 978-1-938267-15-4 (eBook)

Library of Congress Cataloging-in-Publication Data
Juliani, Barbara Miller
Preparing for motherhood : the inside scoop on your new job / Barbara Miller Juliani.
p. cm.
Includes bibliographical references and index.
ISBN-13: 978-1-938267-92-5 (alk. paper)
1. Mothers—Religious life. 2. Motherhood—Religious aspects—Christianity. I. Title.
BV4529.18.J85 2012
248.8'431—dc23

2012026236

Printed in Canada

19 18 17 16 15 14 13 12 1 2 3 4 5

Keisha is pregnant with her first child. She and her husband Tom have done everything they can think of to get ready to welcome their little girl. The baby's room is painted and decorated; they are signed up for birthing classes; they've both read books with lots of helpful information about pregnancy, delivery, and what to expect when they bring home their daughter. But Keisha still has questions. She's heard lots of stories from her friends who already have children, and late at night, when the baby's kicking keeps her awake, she wonders

Will my baby be okay?
Do I have what it takes to be a mom?
What if I do something wrong?
What kinds of problems will we face?
I could never handle what happened to
________________ *. Will that happen to us?*

Samantha is expecting her first child too. She is living with her parents and planning to stay with them while she works, finishes school, and takes care of her new little one. The crib is up in her room; the diapers are bought; and late at night when indigestion keeps her awake, she thinks about the same questions running through Keisha's mind: *Will my baby be okay? Can I cope with being a mom? Who will help me? Who can I count on to help me take care of my baby?*

A few months ago, Ally and John finished all the paperwork for adoption and posted their online profile. Last week they met with a young, pregnant woman who has decided to place her unborn baby boy with them. They have taken seminars on adoption; they have read lots of books; the room is painted blue and decorated with monkeys and basketballs. Late at night when John is sleeping, Ally stays up—too excited and anxious to sleep. Besides all the specific questions and concerns that are special to the adoption process, she wonders, *Will my baby be okay? How will he turn out? Do I have what it takes to be a mom?*

Spiritual Questions Need Spiritual Answers

Every new mom has questions. Reading a book, taking a class, or hearing from friends and relatives can answer some of them—questions like how pregnancy affects your body, how your baby is developing, what to expect at different stages of your pregnancy, and what exactly happens during labor and delivery.

But the questions that keep soon-to-be mothers like Keisha, Samantha, Ally, and perhaps you up at night aren't so easily answered. These questions reflect deeper issues—spiritual issues—and the answers are spiritual as well. Think for a moment. Who can guarantee your safety? Your baby's safety? Who can forgive you if you make a mistake? Who can you count on to guide you and your child through all the ups and downs of life? For the answers to these questions, you need to turn to the One who created you and your child—the One who is powerful enough to knit your child in your womb (Psalm 139:13) *and* powerful enough to calm your anxious heart.

When I was pregnant with my first child, I had many fears and worries. Some of them were specific—Will I have to have a C-section?—and some of them were general—Will I be a good mother? Both kinds of questions filled me with anxiety as I realized how precious my unborn child already was to me and how little I could control. I talked about my fears with my mom because she loved God, and her faith had not only survived raising five children, but had grown through it. When I shared my worries, she looked me in the eye and said, "You have to learn to go to God each time you are anxious." Then she took me to Philippians 4:5–7 and read it out loud to me:

> The Lord is near. Do not be anxious about anything, but in everything, by prayer and petition, with thanksgiving, present your requests to God. And the peace of God, which transcends all understanding, will guard your hearts and your minds in Christ Jesus.

My mom told me to take each worry and present it as a request to the Lord who is near, and then to ask for his peace to guard my mind and heart from fear and worry. I took her advice, and, as I prayed my worries to God, I did experience his peace.

Now, twenty-eighty years later, I can say with certainty that the best way to prepare for your new job of being a mom is to know and trust the Lord who is near. Praying this way is not a magic formula that you use to manage your anxiety. Instead, it's a way to get to know God, to remember he is near, and to learn to trust him with the most precious thing in the world to you—your child.

Learning to trust God with your child is a lifelong project. My children are even more precious to me now than they were as newborns because I've had many years to grow in my love for them. I still worry about them, and I still need to pray my worries back to God. So here are some things I have learned about the Lord who is near. They have given content to my prayers as I welcomed my new little ones and as my husband and I parented them to adulthood.

The Lord Is a Good Shepherd

Before I got pregnant, I didn't really understand how much special care and help I would need when I was pregnant and when I was caring for a newborn. But as soon as morning sickness hit, I realized how needy I was. Not everyone who gets pregnant gets sick, but you will experience weakness in some way because pregnancy and caring for a newborn bring with them a physical and emotional vulnerability. Since God made you, he already knows this about you. He promises to take special care of you and your baby during this time. Here is his promise to you:

> He tends his flock like a shepherd:
> He gathers the lambs in his arms
> and carries them close to his heart;
> he gently leads those that have young.
> (Isaiah 40:11)

When you feel physically and emotionally depleted, when you struggle to get through the day or sleep through the night, remember that you have a good shepherd who has promised to gently lead you. You are not the only one carrying your child; God is carrying your little one "close to his heart." He has given you the job of shepherding and caring for a new life, but he hasn't left you on your own. He is watching over you and your child. He is helping you through each day.

Jesus calls himself "the Good Shepherd." He promises that he knows and calls each of his sheep by name (John 10:1–18). He knows you; he knows your child (and your child's name even if you haven't decided yet!). It is Jesus who is carrying you and your child close to his heart.

The most important thing for you to remember about your Good Shepherd is that he lays down his life for his sheep (John 10:11, 15). You might have already noticed that you are willing to do almost anything to make sure that your child is safe and healthy. Perhaps you have already changed your diet or given up habits that might negatively impact your child's health.

But Jesus' love for his sheep goes further than that. He loves you so much that he gave up his own life so that you might live with him forever.

Your fears for your child might seem irrational at times, but they are rooted in the very real brokenness of this world. You know that things are not the way they should be, and you don't want your child to experience any suffering. If you are honest with yourself, you also know that you aren't always the way *you* should be. From talking with your friends and reading about how to prepare for motherhood, you might be wondering if you have what it takes to learn this new job, to take care of another human being 24/7. Perhaps you are worrying about the mistakes you might make as a mom and how they will affect your child.

Our mistakes and failures are part of the brokenness of the world as well, but the good news is that when Jesus, our Good Shepherd, laid down his life for his sheep, his death bought forgiveness and new life for those who trust in him. Because Jesus died and was raised from the dead to live forever, you can be sure of these things when you put your trust in him:

1. You can be sure that nothing that happens to you or your child can separate you from God's love (Romans 8:31–39).
2. You can be sure that when you make a mistake in parenting your child you can go to

God and ask for forgiveness, and he will freely forgive you (Romans 8:1–2).

3. You can be sure that none of the brokenness of this world and none of the mistakes you make can stop God's love from being poured out on you and your child, because *all* things work together for the good of those who love God (Romans 8:28).

If you find yourself doubting these truths, turn to John 10 and Romans 8 and read them all the way through. Read one chapter in the morning and one chapter at night until these truths sink deep into your heart and soul. Remember each day that Jesus is your Good Shepherd, who is gently leading you and carrying you and your child. In him you and your child will find forgiveness, love, life, and every good thing.

Trusting Your Child's Future to Your Good Shepherd

Every mom wonders how her child will turn out. When you are pregnant or waiting to adopt, you don't have too much data to help you. A sonogram or a picture might tell you the shape of her face or his size. You might know your child's sex by now (something that back in the day was a subject for much speculation). You can guess at your baby's personality by how active he is, but right now almost everything about your child is just that—a guess.

There's a lot you don't know right now, but one thing I can guarantee: when you meet your child for the first time, you will think that he or she is pretty special. And you will want your special child to have an exceptional future. Perhaps you already have dreams for your child. Perhaps you hope she avoids some of your mistakes or has successes you've never had. My husband's immigrant parents dreamed he would go to college and have opportunities that weren't available to them.

God has entrusted you and your husband with helping your child discover God's purposes for her life. That will be a process that spans her childhood and extends into adulthood. But be assured that your child does have unique gifts that God wants to use in his kingdom. As you point your child to God's unique purposes, her life will be filled with adventure and significance.

Guiding your child this way starts with you entrusting your child—and the dreams you have for her—back to God. The Bible has plenty of stories about parents who trusted their children to God in the midst of the most difficult circumstances. Think about Abraham and Isaac (Genesis 22), Moses' mother and father (Exodus 1 and 2), Hannah and little Samuel (1 Samuel 1), Elizabeth and John (Luke 1), and Mary and Jesus (Luke 2). In every case, their trust in God led to two amazing things: blessing for their child, and their child being an important part of God's kingdom.

Moses' Mother

I often think about one of those stories—the story of Moses and his parents—when I'm struggling to trust God with my children. You can read the whole story in Exodus 1 and 2, but here's a summary: Moses was born during a horrific time in the history of God's people. The Hebrews had been slaves in Egypt for hundreds of years. When Moses' mother was pregnant with him, things were going from bad to worse. The king of Egypt (the Pharaoh) wanted to control the population of the Hebrew slaves so he told the midwives to throw all the newborn Hebrew boys into the Nile River.

Imagine how Moses' parents must have felt when his mother delivered a baby boy. Were they full of fear and despair? That probably would have been my response, but the book of Hebrews gives us a different picture. Like most new parents, they saw that their little boy was "no ordinary child" and they were not afraid of the king or his power to have their baby killed (Hebrews 11:23). Instead, they trusted the God who had given them their son and, by faith, they hid Moses and then put him in a waterproof basket, a tiny ark, to float on the Nile River. That might seem like the death of their dreams and hopes for their little one, but it was really just the beginning of what God was going to do to prepare Moses to lead his people out of slavery to freedom. Their act of faith, their willingness to entrust back to God his most precious gift to them, led to freedom for millions of people.

One day, as I was worrying about the future of my children, I started to think about Moses' mom. What was it like putting together that little ark for her newborn son? I realized that what she did by faith God was calling me to do as well—to actively trust him with the lives of my children. As I thought about these things, I wrote this poem.

Moses' Mother

If she, by faith,
Could weave a small basket,
Carefully coat it with pitch,
And place her not-so-ordinary newborn
In the homemade ark,
Letting the water carry him away,

Then perhaps we also, by faith,
Could trust the water and the blood
To keep us and our not-so-ordinary children
Safe.[1]

Compared to us, Moses' mother knew so little about God. She had heard the stories of how God had called their ancestors to be his special people. She knew that God had brought them to Egypt for a purpose 500 years earlier, but they had been slaves for a long time. Yet still, by faith, she trusted her son to God's good care. She trusted God to keep her son safe.

Today we know so much more about the way God works. Not only do we have the stories of the exodus—the parting of the Red Sea, the bread from heaven, the water from the rock—but we also have the rest of the story. We know that Jesus, our Good Shepherd, came to lead his people out of slavery and death. We know he laid down his life and then took it up again. We know that turning to him in repentance and faith gives us eternal life. We know that the God we worship has defeated death. We have the historical truths of Christ's death and resurrection to base our faith on.

If Moses' mother could trust the God she knew so little about with her not-so-ordinary child, then certainly it is possible for us to trust God with our not-so-ordinary children. Of course, God isn't calling you and me to put our children in a little basket on large river. But he is calling us, like Moses' mother, to actively trust him with our children's lives and futures. This will mean something different for each of us. But we will all need the same faith that God gave to Moses' mother to live out this essential part of our new job.

Faith doesn't come automatically. It is a gift we have to ask Jesus for throughout our parenting years (Luke 11:9–10). When I look back at my twenty-eight years of parenting four children, my only regret is how often I lived in unbelief and fear instead of in faith and freedom. I have learned through the years to ask God every day for the faith to entrust my children to him. You can learn that lesson now, before your child is in your arms. Your best gift to your new little one will be to live by faith in the God who can keep your child safe and give him a life of meaning and significance.

Living by Faith through the Arrival of Your Child

Even though you are not facing the same difficulties as Moses' mother, you are facing the arrival of your child. If you are pregnant, you are waiting to go through labor and delivery. If you are adopting a child, welcoming your child (and the journey to that moment) is a momentous occasion full of emotional ups and downs. Since many people are not shy about sharing scary stories about these events, I'm sure you have heard a few. Most likely you also have your own set of worries and fears about the arrival of your child. So this is a good time to actively live by faith—to go over all the truths you know about your Good Shepherd and his care for you and your child.

My sister-in-law Jill gave me some advice when I was pregnant with my first that helped me live by faith through the births of my four children. She already had four children, so I asked her about everything. I was taking birthing classes, but I wanted to know what else I could do to prepare for labor. Jill told me that before the birth of each of her children she picked a psalm to memorize and pray through for them—starting with labor.

The psalm she picked for the birth of her fourth child was Psalm 121. Since I wasn't too familiar with the Psalms, I chose that one as well. It turned out to be the perfect psalm for the delivery of my son. It was short enough to memorize easily; it fit the long labor I experienced that stretched from the day through the night ("the sun will not harm you by day, nor the moon by night," v. 6); it comforted me with the knowledge that even when my exhausted husband fell asleep, God was still awake, watching and keeping me ("he who watches over you will not slumber; indeed, he who watches over Israel will neither slumber or sleep," vv. 3–4). Amid the complications I experienced, it reminded me that God had promised no harm would come to us ("The Lord will keep you from all harm—he will watch over your life," v. 7).

I still pray Psalm 121 for my twenty-eight-year-old son, his wife, and his three-year-old daughter and baby son. And, if I get the chance, I share with every new mom I talk with how God helped me as I prayed a psalm through each of my children's arrivals. Now would be a great time for you to pick a psalm to start praying for your child, through his arrival and the rest of his life as well. You can use Psalm 121, or Psalm 23 (all about our Good Shepherd), or Psalm 139 (a great way to remind yourself that God is holding your child fast now and forever).

Living by Faith as You Learn a New Job

It might seem like getting your child safely home is the biggest project (and it is a big project!), but really the fun is just beginning. Now you start to really learn your new job—being a mom. As with any other new job, you will realize that there is a lot to learn in a short time. But being a mom is different from any other job you have had because 1) God has entrusted you with the care of a little, completely helpless, and very precious human, and 2) your job is 24/7. Having that much responsibility around the clock is challenging for new moms. (And not just the first time you welcome a little one into your home. I was overwhelmed every time I brought a baby home!)

The best way to learn is while you are doing your new job, but there are a few things to keep in mind now that will help as you learn how to care for your little one.

Living by Faith through the "Firsts"

There will be many "firsts" in the days after you bring your child home: the first car ride, the first night at home, the first time you are home alone with your newborn, the first time your husband (or other caregiver) is home alone with your baby, the first bath, the first trip out of the house (and managing the baby's schedule so you can actually leave), and so on. Don't be surprised if each one of these occasions feels a bit overwhelming. And don't forget that your Good Shepherd is with you through every first. You are not learning this big, new job on your own. You have Jesus with you, watching over you and your little one. Ask him to help you, to protect your new child, and to guide you in learning how to care for her.

If you are married, then a big new first will be your husband and you parenting your family together. This can be a wonderful time. I remember my husband telling me that after he left the hospital after the birth of our first child how he was filled with joy and thankfulness that God had given him not only a wife, but also a child to love and care for. But, of course, it can also be a stressful time as you and your husband adjust to being a family, to the time and attention that a newborn takes (particularly from you), and to anxieties that come as you face so many firsts together.

Remember to include your husband in parenting—even parenting a newborn. Give him ways to participate with you in taking care of your little one. It will be easy for him to feel a bit marginalized by all the care your newborn needs. So, even in the stress of caring for a new life, make sure your husband knows you still love and care for him. Most importantly, give your husband grace as he also goes through the adjustments that parenthood brings. Just like you, he is learning what it means to be responsible for a new life. Just like you, his life is full of firsts. Talk honestly with him about struggles and fears you are both encountering. Just as you go to God with your worries, go to your husband as well so you can each know the other's burdens and pray with and for each other and your new baby. Expect a period of adjustment. But also expect that God will use your new family to grow you closer to him and to each other.

Living by Faith through Weakness

Giving birth and bringing a newborn home from the hospital brings physical and emotional weakness into your life. Labor and delivery leaves you sore and tired. Your fluctuating hormones affect your emotions. And your baby's need to eat every few hours means you are sleep-deprived as well. It will be easy to respond to weakness with frustration or discouragement. You can pray about these things now and ask your Good Shepherd to help you respond in faith to weakness. Turning to Christ in your weakness will be a great blessing in your life because it will teach you to depend on him every moment of every day. That's what living by faith is all about.

Please say "yes" to the help you are offered when you come home with your child. My tendency is to say, "I can do it myself," but this is not the time for self-sufficiency or proving that you already know how to be a mom. (That's what God calls pride, and it's the opposite of living by faith.) Instead, it's a time to admit you need help and say "yes" to those who offer. Let your husband (or other caregiver) help you with your baby. If someone offers to bring you meals, say "yes."

If your mother and mother-in-law are present and available, allow them to come and help you. It's okay to admit that you don't know what you are doing and to ask for advice.

Ask Jesus to give you patience through this time of weakness—with your recovery, with the ups and downs of your emotions, with those who help you and don't do things exactly the way you would like, and with yourself as you learn step-by-step your new job of being a 24/7 mother.

Living by Faith with Uncertainty

One of the most challenging parts of your new job is learning to manage your baby's eating and sleeping schedule. The challenging part is that they don't really have one! Although I knew this, it was still shocking to me to arrive home with a newborn and realize I was on call 24/7. Every other job I'd worked had a beginning time and ending time, but not caring for my baby. Before the arrival of my first child, I could arrange my life the way I thought best. After his arrival, his needs ordered my days. That was a big adjustment for me. Just when I thought he was going to nap (because he had napped before at that time), he was up. Just when I thought we had gotten his eating on a predictable schedule, he went through a growth spurt. And so it goes with a newborn, a toddler, and really any child. Their needs have priority over yours, and their needs aren't always predictable.

There are many books written on how to manage your baby's schedule. And every family and every baby are unique, so navigating your way through that process will be unique to your family and your child. But there aren't so many things written on how to deal with the constant pressure of your child's uncertain schedule. I found that, like everything else, this challenge needed to be met by faith. I had to remember every moment of every day that although it seemed like my little one was in charge of my life, really God was (and is) in charge of every moment of every day.

Every day I had to remember the truth that God's plans were best because he is good and everything he does is good (Psalm 119:68). And then I had to keep giving back to him my plans for each day. When I was upset, I prayed one phrase again and again, "My times are in your hands" (Psalm 31:15). I prayed that phrase through missed naps, teething and sickness that kept us up at night, diapers that needed changing just as I was finally ready to walk out the door, skinned knees, hospital visits to set broken bones—there have been so many opportunities in the last twenty-eight years to turn to God and give him my plans for my days and nights. Really, this is a one-size-fits-all prayer that can change any frustrating situation into an opportunity to grow in your trust in God's care, God's plans, and his way of ordering your days (and nights).

Motherhood Is a Gift—Not a Competitive Sport

You've probably already noticed that moms and moms-to-be are, like humans everywhere, competitive people. So it's natural that, as you start your new job, you will be looking at what others are doing and they will be looking at you. You will notice in yourself and other moms a tendency to compete over such things as how well your baby sleeps and eats, how fast he or she grows, and how fast you lose your baby weight. The list is endless of things we are either happy we do better than someone else or worried we haven't done as well. And when you add children into the mix, the intensity of the competition seems to ratchet up a few more notches.

I remember that during the first year of my oldest son's life, I was worried that his development was delayed. Of course, now he is twenty-eight and just fine. But I had a friend whose little girl was born a few months before him, and it seemed that she did everything faster than my son. She turned over, crawled, walked, babbled, said first words, and did everything else earlier than he did. Naturally—she was a girl! (At least in our family, our daughter did everything sooner than our three sons.) Since he was my first, I worried constantly about his development. But, on the other hand, my son was a great sleeper. He slept through the night early, and that made me feel like a great mother—and just a little bit better than those mothers whose babies were still getting up at night. That lasted until I had another child who struggled to sleep through the night. Then I felt like a terrible mother!

Do you see what a trap all of this is? When you treat motherhood as a competition, you are bound to either think you are better than someone else or be upset that somehow you are worse. How much better to think about being a mom the way God tells us to think about everything—as a gift. Psalm 127:3 tells us that children are a gift from God. And the apostle Paul reminds us not to boast about our gifts when he says, "For who makes you different from anyone else? What do you have that you did not receive? And if you did receive it, why do you boast as though you did not?" (1 Corinthians 4:7). So if your child happens to shine in one area, that is a gift from God. If you happen to shine as a mother in one area, that is a gift from God too. And the best (and polite) response to getting a gift is to be thankful to God, and then to use your strength to help to others (Romans 15:1).

If you feel weak in an area, there is no shame in that because motherhood is not a competitive sport! It's okay to admit you are weak to God and to others. You can ask for help when you are overwhelmed by taking care of a child 24/7. And the truth is that every mom has days when it seems like everything is going wrong. The Bible tells us that we all stumble and fall in many ways (James 3:2). You will feel this keenly as a mother. But you do have a Savior. You do have One who never stumbled and fell, but who does understand weakness. You can go to him for forgiveness and help. He is your Good Shepherd. He loves you and wants to help you. He will freely forgive and freely help. And because you can go to him without fear, you can also admit your weaknesses to others without fear and ask them for help and prayer.

Go to Jesus with Everything, Every Day

No small minibook can answer all the specific questions and concerns you have as you prepare for motherhood. But my hope is that you will remember that Jesus, your Good Shepherd, walks with you through this new challenge, and that he will never leave you or forsake you. Jesus never fails. He will not fail you. He will not fail your child.

As you, by faith, go to him every day for forgiveness, help, guidance, and strength, he will be with you. Putting all your faith in him is the key to motherhood (and life). I promise that you will not be disappointed by putting your faith in Jesus. And one day you will look back at these years and, despite all of the challenges, what you will remember best is that Jesus was with you every step of the way—watching, keeping, and holding you and your family fast.

Endnotes

1. Barbara Miller Juliani, "Moses' Mother," copyright 2008.